CHILDREN'S NEW TESTAMENT
BIBLE STORIES

FEATURING Coptic ILLUSTRATIONS

Fr. Tadros Yacoub Malaty

Children's New Testament Bible Stories, Featuring Coptic Illustrations

Copyright © 2018 by Fr. Tadros Yacoub Malaty

Illustrations by Tasony Sawsan

All rights reserved.

Designed & Published by:
St. Mary & St. Moses Abbey Press
101 S. Vista Dr., Sandia, TX 78383
stmabbeypress.com

Library of Congress Control Number: 2018936544

Children's New Testament Bible Stories

Featuring Coptic Illustrations

Foreword

Dear Reader,

Between your hands is one of a series of two books (Old and New Testament) made for easy daily readings of biblical stories with your child. The Holy Bible delivers divine wisdom that provides enlightenment to all people and all ages.

Whoever reads the Holy Bible with the spirit of piety strives to know God and experience His abundant love for all humankind.

1. Many verses were kept unchanged so that your child becomes familiar with them.

2. For your young child, read what is written but in everyday language so that the child can easily follow along. As your child grows, allow him or her to read the book as it is written providing explanations so that the child can gradually read the Holy Bible without assistance.

His Grace Bishop Angaelos of London, England suggested that we follow the Coptic style for our illustrations so that our children experience the spiritual connotations of the icons.

Would you please read me this book!
The Evangelists

Our Lord Jesus called men who were close to Him to be His disciples and friends. We are Matthew, Mark, Luke, and John and the Church refers to us as the "Evangelists" because we wrote the four accounts of the Holy Gospel with guidance from the Holy Spirit.

The word, "gospel," means to "announce good news," and the word, "Evangelist," means "a missionary writer of the story of our Lord Jesus." The Evangelists of the Holy Gospel bring joy to people in Christ who opened to us the doors of heaven through the cross. This is so that we enter and join the angels, the archangels, and all the heavenly hosts to praise God and to enjoy eternal glory.

We have written our four accounts of the Holy Gospel, which are the first four books in the New Testament.

Saint Matthew

My name is Matthew. I am one of the disciples of our Lord Jesus Christ. Led by the Holy Spirit, I wrote the Gospel according to Matthew to my brothers and sisters the Jews—the people of Israel—so that they know that Jesus was a descendant of King David. I made more references to prophecies from the Old Testament than any other account of the Holy Gospel.

Before I met our Lord Jesus, I worked as a tax collector collecting taxes for the Roman Empire. I wanted to be very rich. I pressured people to pay more than their fair share of taxes and keep the extra for myself. One day, while sitting at the tax collection agency, our Lord Jesus walked by me and said, "Follow me." I got up and followed Him. Then, I invited Jesus to a feast at my home with other tax collectors and sinners. We all sat around Jesus and enjoyed His presence among us. Jewish leaders, scribes, and Pharisees were angry that Jesus sat and ate with us.

They said to the disciples, "Why does your teacher eat with tax collectors and sinners?"

When our Lord heard that, He replied, "Those who are well have no need for a physician but those who are sick. I came not to call the righteous, but sinners to repentance."

Prayer: My Lord Jesus, You sat and ate with tax collectors because sinners need to hear You more than those who truly know You. Lord, please stay in the hearts of all people.

Saint Mark

My name is John Mark, the cousin of Saint Barnabas, who accompanied Saint Paul the Apostle, and a relative of Saint Peter the Apostle who considered me his son.

With guidance from the Holy Spirit, I wrote the Holy Gospel according to Mark to my Roman brothers and sisters who were in the Roman Empire so that they know that our Lord Jesus came to serve not only the Jews, but also the whole world. He loves everyone and was crucified to save all people. He wants everyone to enter heaven.

Prayer: Thank You, God, for opening the doors of heaven to all nations and people.

Saint Luke

My name is Luke and I am the only Gentile (non-Jew) among the Evangelists. I was not among God's chosen people. I worked as a doctor and, you may remember, that I traveled with Paul the Apostle and learned so much from him. We traveled together to many places and talked to people about our Lord Jesus—the marvelous friend to all believers.

With guidance from the Holy Spirit, I wrote the Holy Gospel according to Luke to those who were educated in the Greek language because it was the most widely used language in the world, especially in the East. I wanted people to know the truth about our Savior Jesus.

With the guidance of the Holy Spirit, I also wrote the Book of Acts. In it, I wrote about the early work of the disciples and apostles after the ascension of our Lord Jesus to heaven and the descent of the Holy Spirit. I also wrote accounts of the early missionary trips, particularly those of Saint Paul the Apostle, so that everyone knows that the Holy Spirits leads the Church of Christ.

Prayer: Grant me, Lord, to be proud of Your friendship and love for all people.

Saint John

My name is John, and I am one of the disciples of our Lord Jesus. I was very close to Him and earned the label, "the disciple whom Jesus loved." When our Savior Jesus was dying on the cross, He asked me to take care of His mother, the Virgin Saint Mary.

Our Lord Jesus called my brother, James, and I, the "sons of thunder." My father's name was Zebedee, not thunder, but the Lord Jesus called us "sons of thunder" because of our nature and eagerness to attract people to our Savior Jesus Christ.

I wanted all people to believe in our Lord Jesus because He is the Son of God, the Word of God, and to accept Him as their Savior.

Guided by the Holy Spirit, I wrote my account of the Holy Gospel to all believers so that they all know that Jesus is God, the Word, and one with the Father who is able to make us children of God.

Prayer: Thank you, Lord, for sending Matthew, the missionary, so that we know that You are Christ, about whom the prophets prophesied, and for sending the apostle Mark so that we know that You came down to serve all humans, and for sending the apostle Luke so that we know that You are our divine friend, and for sending the apostle John so that we learn that You are the Son of God, and that through Your grace we become children of God.

The Angel's Announcement to Zachariah the Priest
Luke 1

My name is Zachariah. I am a priest and my wife is Elizabeth. We grew old and did not have any children. While serving at the altar and praying, an angel came to me and told me that I will have a son who will be called John and many people will be happy with his birth, as he will prepare the way to receive our Lord Jesus for whom humans have been waiting.

I did not believe what I saw and heard, so the angel said, "I am Gabriel! I stand in God's presence. God sent me to tell you this good news. Because you did not believe what I said, you will be unable to speak until the day this happens. Everything will come true at the right time."

A few days later, I completed my service in the sanctuary in silence, I returned to my home, and my wife Elizabeth became pregnant. She was so happy, but she did not meet anyone for five months because she was embarrassed due to her old age.

Question: What could you tell people about Jesus Christ and about His promises? Did He keep His promise to Zachariah?

The Angel Gabriel's Announcement to the Virgin Mary
ᗡ Luke 1 ᗢ

I am Mary, a poor young girl in a small village called Nazareth. I did not want to get married because I preferred to spend all my life serving the Lord with Joseph the Carpenter.

God sent Gabriel the angel to deliver a very important message to me. At first, I was very afraid, but the angel comforted me and said, "Rejoice, highly favored one (full of grace), the Lord is with you." The angel told me that God has chosen me to be the mother of His Son, the Word of God, and our Lord Jesus. I said to the angel, "May it be to me as you have said."

I was very happy because I was going to become the mother of Jesus Christ the Savior, mother of God. I rejoiced and sang hymns to thank the Lord.

Question: What did the angel Gabriel say to the virgin Saint Mary?

The Birth of Our Lord, Jesus
Luke 2

Caesar, the emperor of Rome who ruled the world, issued a decree that all people go back to the place of their birth to register their names in a census so that he could collect taxes. We (Mary and Joseph) left Galilee, a city in Nazareth, for Bethlehem on a long journey that lasted three days by foot. There were many people there to register, so when we went to the inn to get a room, there were none available. The owner of the inn saw how tired I was from the long journey and told us to stay at his cattle barn.

That was the night of the birth of my Son, Jesus, the only Son of God. I wrapped Him in swaddling clothes and laid Him in a manger. A manger is where straw and food for the cattle and other animals are kept. During the night, some shepherds came and told us an incredible story. They said that while they were keeping watch over their flock at night, an angel of the Lord appeared and stood before them. The glory of the Lord shone around them. They were frightened. The angel said to them, "Do not be afraid. I bring you good news that will cause great joy for all the people. Today, in the town of David, a Savior has been born to you; He is the Messiah, the Lord." Suddenly, a great company of heavenly host appeared praising God and saying, "Glory to God in the highest heaven, and peace to His people of earth." They marveled and rushed to Bethlehem to worship the Child.

I kept all these words and pondered them in my heart.

My Son Jesus Christ is the King of kings, although He was not born in a mansion, but was born and began His earthly life in a manger. He slept on straw that was kept for the cattle so that all people see that He came for all people, rich and poor. For you, He was born in a manger.

Prayer: Thank you, Lord, for coming down for me and for all my brothers and sisters who are rich and poor.

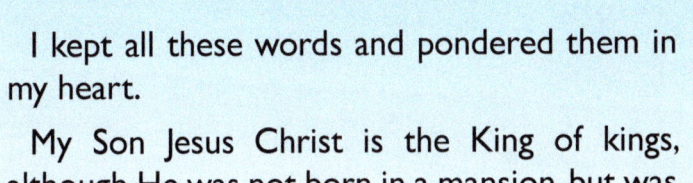

Wise Men from the East
Matthew 2

We are called the Magi, or wise men, and we live in the East (in the area of Iran). We study astronomy and saw a wondrous star, so we followed it because we learned that a star would appear when the King of the Jews is born.

We are not Jews, but we know that He loves all people without any favoritism. We left our country in a great procession seeking the Newborn, the great King.

After many days and nights, we went to Bethlehem where a great crowd gathered around us asking us about the reason for our visit. We told them that we left our homes and came to worship the Child, the great King. No one told us of the place of His birth.

When Herod the king heard about this, he became disturbed because there were no babies born in his castle. So, he requested that we visit him along with the priests and scribes who told him that a prophet had prophesied that Christ will be born in Bethlehem. We left the castle after we were asked to return to let him know where the Child was born so that he, too, can go and worship Him. The star led us to the small town of Bethlehem.

We know that the Child Jesus is a great King and, therefore, we brought Him gifts—gold, frankincense, and myrrh: (1) gold, because He is King, (2) frankincense, because He is the heavenly High Priest, and (3) myrrh, because He will suffer and be crucified for us.

The angel of the Lord appeared to Saint Joseph and told him to take the Baby and His mother to Egypt so that Isaiah's prophecy in Chapter 19 in the Old Testament is fulfilled: "Blessed is Egypt My people."

Prayer: My Lord Jesus, I love you. Accept my heart as a gift to you so that you can dwell in it. My Lord Jesus, you came to Egypt and blessed it and established Your Church there and similarly blessed the Church around the world.

The Infant Jesus at the Temple
Luke 2

I am Simeon, an elderly man. I waited many years to see the anticipated Christ, the Son of God, who was born to a virgin. God led me to the temple where Saint Mary came in with the infant Lord Jesus. I saw the angels worship Him and was overjoyed. I took Him in my arms saying, "Lord, now You are letting Your servant depart in peace according to Your word; for my eyes have seen Your salvation which You have prepared before the face of all peoples, a light to bring revelation to the Gentiles, and the glory of Your people Israel."

Question: Are you waiting to see our Lord Jesus on the clouds during His Second Coming?

Our Lord Jesus Teaches the Scribes and Teachers in the Temple
Luke 2

I am Joseph, the fiancé of the virgin, Saint Mary. We went back to our home in Nazareth with our Lord and Savior Jesus. As our Lord Jesus grew, He helped us. He was really exceptional. Each year, we went to Jerusalem during Passover with our relatives and acquaintances. We would stay there a few days, then return to our hometown. When Jesus turned twelve years of age, He did something that amazed us. We went to Jerusalem for the Passover. When celebrations ended, we began our journey back. After spending a whole day on the road, we realized that Jesus was not with us. We checked with our family and friends, but we could not find Him. We returned to Jerusalem searching for Him everywhere.

Finally, we found Him in the Temple sitting among great knowledgeable teachers, listening to them and asking questions. They were so fascinated by Him, as they found Him to be very wise. This is not surprising, for He knows everything about the Father because He is the Son of God. When we saw Him, we were surprised. I (his mother) said to Him, "Son, why have you treated us like this? Your father and I have been anxiously searching for You."

Jesus answered her, "Why were you searching for Me? Did you not know I had to be in my Father's house?" We did not understand that He was on a special mission, which is saving the world on the cross. Then we returned to our house in Nazareth and watched Him grow in wisdom, stature, and grace.

Prayer: My Lord Jesus, how I long to hear Your voice when You teach me and give me the desire to help my parents the way You did!

The Baptism of Our Lord Jesus
Luke 3

My name is John the Baptist. I preached near the Jordan River. I asked people to stop doing the evil things that saddened God.

Many people were repentant for what they had done and I baptized them in the river so that they could start a new life in purity.

Our Lord Jesus came to the river and asked me to baptize Him also. I was astonished because He was my Lord and did not need baptism; rather, I needed to be baptized by Him.

The heaven was opened and the Holy Spirit descended upon Him like a bright beautiful dove and I heard a voice from heaven saying, "This is my Son, whom I love; with Him I am well pleased."

He gave us baptism so we can become children of God.

Prayer: Thank You, Lord, for through Your Holy Spirit in the baptistery basin, I became Your child.

Temptation of our Lord Jesus
Luke 4

When our Lord Jesus turned thirty years of age, He began serving the people. At the beginning, He went to the desert to pray and stayed forty days. He did not eat anything during that time. Instead, He fasted, but became hungry toward the end. It was then that Satan came to tempt Him. He asked our Lord Jesus three difficult questions from the Holy Bible.

Satan said to Him, "If You are the Son of God, tell this rock to become bread."

Jesus responded with biblical phrases, saying, "It is written: 'Man shall not live by bread alone, but by every word that comes from the mouth of God.'"

Then Satan took him to a very high mountain and showed him all the kingdoms of the world and said to Him, "All this I will give You if You will bow down and worship me."

Jesus answered him, saying, "Away from Me, Satan! For it is written: 'Worship the Lord you God, and serve Him only.'"

A third time, Satan took Jesus and had Him stand on the highest point of the temple and said to Him, "If you are the Son of God, throw yourself down for it is written: 'He will command His angels concerning You, and they will lift You up in their hands, so that You will not strike Your foot against a stone.'"

Jesus replied, "It is also written: 'Do not put the Lord Your God to the test.'"

Our Lord Jesus pushed Satan away by saying that the Bible tells us, "Do not put the Lord Your God to the test."

Finally, Satan gave up on his attempts to tempt our Lord Jesus for the time being. Angels came to serve our Lord Jesus Christ.

Our Lord Jesus Goes to a Wedding
John 2

One day, our Lord Jesus went to attend a wedding at Cana in Galilee.

Saint Mary noticed that the wine was finished, so she told her Son. Our Lord Jesus told the servants, "Fill the jars with water." They did what He asked of them. The water turned into good wine, but he did not drink.

This was the first miracle our Lord Jesus performed.

Prayer: My Lord, enter into my heart so that I am happy with Your presence in me.

33

Our Lord Jesus Invites Four Fishermen
John 1

One day, our Lord Jesus saw four fishermen repairing their nets. Their names were Simon Peter, Andrew, James, and John.

Our Lord Jesus said to them, "Follow Me! I will teach you how to fish for people instead of fish."

They were very happy and followed our Lord Jesus because they wanted all people to enjoy knowing Jesus Christ.

Our Lord Jesus chose twelve men (disciples) who joined Him everywhere He went and witnessed Him perform many miracles. He healed the sick, gave sight to the blind, and made the paralyzed able to walk. He taught them about the Father and the kingdom of heaven because He fills heaven and earth.

Question: Would you like to become a disciple of our Lord Jesus, telling people about Him and about His love for all humanity?

Our Lord Jesus with Fishermen
Luke 5

Our Lord Jesus entered the fishing boat where fishermen spent the whole night trying to catch fish and did not catch one fish.

Our Lord Jesus asked them to move a little farther from the shore and cast their nets in the water.

Because of their experience, the fishermen knew that spot was not suitable for fishing, but they obeyed anyway and threw their nets according to His word. This time, they caught so much fish that their nets began to tear. The fishermen were amazed and decided to follow Him because they saw that He could do things others could not do.

Question: Why did the fishermen obey our Lord Jesus?

Our Lord Jesus, the Good Teacher, Teaches the Multitudes
Matthew 5–7

Our Lord Jesus began to travel to many towns and villages along with His disciples. He told people many marvelous stories in order to make the world a better place and to bring joy to His children.

One of those days, He saw the crowds and went to the mountain to have a pleasant time joined by His beloved disciples. There, He taught everyone how to walk in everlasting joy and to be blessed and become the children of light: "Blessed are the poor in spirit, for theirs is the kingdom of heaven…. Blessed are the merciful, for they will be shown mercy. Blessed ate the pure in heart, for they will see God. Blessed are the peacemakers, for they will be called children of God…. Blessed are you when people insult you, persecute you…. Rejoice and be very glad, because great is our reward in heaven."

He also taught us how to speak with our heavenly Father with love and submissiveness:

"Our Father who art in heaven … Amen"

Many people came to Him with all types of illnesses and He healed them.

Question: When you pray, "Our Father who art in heaven," do you feel that you are talking to your heavenly Father and that God dwells in your heart?

Our Lord Jesus with Nicodemus
John 3

My name is Nicodemus. I paid a visit to Jesus at night because I was afraid of the Jews. I wanted to go to heaven, and I wanted to ask Him how to get there.

Our Lord told me that God loves all people and that is why He sent His only Son to die for them. He also told me that I needed a new life from God and that I must be born again to go to heaven.

I heard Him carefully, but I found great difficulty in understanding what He meant.

However, now I know that every man or woman who believes in the Lord Jesus, the Son of God, and is baptized by water and Spirit also becomes the child of God and can enter into the kingdom of heaven.

Do you know the name of the Son of God? It is Jesus.

Our Lord Jesus Christ Meets the Samaritan Woman at Jacob's Well
John 4

I am the Samaritan woman. I was by Jacob's well in Samaria when our Lord Jesus arrived from a long trip and was thirsty. He sat at the edge of the well and asked me to give Him some water to drink. I was surprised because I knew the Jews hated us, the Samaritans, since we have combined the worship of the only living God with pagan practices.

He told me the Father sent Him and if I drink from the water that He has, I will never thirst again. He also told me that He could give me something better than water: He can give me a happy life with God.

The Lord also told me many things I had not heard of before, so I told Him that He must be the awaited Messiah. He answered, "I am He," and told me that He has come to save the world.

I believed in our Lord Jesus and I loved Him. I went into the city and told everybody about Him, so they all came happy to listen to Him. They also believed in Him and loved Him.

Question: What can our Lord Jesus give this woman?

Our Lord Jesus Asks Us to Be Nice
Matthew 5

Our Lord Jesus wants us to be nice to everybody. He does not want us to fight or to be angry.

He wants us to pray for all people, even the mean ones, so they can become nice too.

He gave us the golden rule, "Do unto others as you would have them do unto you."

Question: What can you do to help another person?

Our Lord Jesus with the Paralyzed Man
Luke 5

One day, I heard that our Lord Jesus was in town teaching. Many people surrounded Him and I am a paralyzed man, unable to move. Four of my friends carried me in my bed to the house where our Lord was, but there was a problem; we could not reach our Lord Jesus because of the crowds.

My friends carried me to the roof, which was made of boards. They moved some of the boards to the side to clear a hole where they lowered me in my bed in the middle of the room right in front of the Lord. The people surrounding our Lord Jesus were surprised to see a bed lowered from the roof in front of Him. Our Lord saw the faith of my friends, so He looked at me and said, "Your sins are forgiven," but the leaders of the Jews did not like that. Our Lord knew what they were thinking in their hearts: "Who can forgive sins but God alone?"

Then, Jesus asked them why they think like this in their hearts: "Which is easier to say, 'Your sins are forgiven you' or to say 'rise up and walk?'" When no one answered Him, He said that he would do that so that they may know that He has the power to forgive sins and, then, He told me to get up, carry my bed, and go to my home. Immediately, I got up and walked and everyone glorified God saying, "We have seen strange things today!"

The Shepherd Looks for the Lost Sheep
Luke 15

Our Lord told us many great and beautiful stories, and we love those stories. Here is one of them.

There was a good shepherd who had one hundred sheep. He tended to his lambs night and day and gave each lamb a name. One day, he noticed that one of his sheep was missing. Immediately, the shepherd went to search for his lost lamb. Where would it be? He kept looking here and there, in the valleys, and on the hills, and among the thorns. Finally, he found his lost lamb; so, he carried it and put it on his shoulders until he brought it home. The shepherd, then, invited his friends and told them to come and celebrate with him because he has found his lost lamb.

God also rejoices when a person who sinned comes back to Him and repents. The angels, who are God's friends, also rejoice with Him.

You are like a little lamb and our Lord Jesus knows you and knows your name. He misses you and cannot stand living without you because He loves you.

Exercise: Pray for yourself and for those who sin that they may repent and return to God.

The Story of the Two New Homes
Matthew 7; Luke 6

Our Lord Jesus told us another story about two men. Each of them decided to build a new home.

The first man built his house on the soft sand without setting a deep foundation underneath it, while the second man built his house on a solid rock.

One day, a big storm blew. The rain poured down, and the water started to rise. The house that was built on sand fell and broke down, but the house that was built on solid rock stood strong and did not shake.

Our Lord Jesus explained that those who listen to His words and do as He says are like the man who built his house on solid rock.

Question: How do you build your house? Do you build your house on a rock? Who is the rock?

The Story of the Nice Father
Luke 15

Our Lord Jesus told us another story about a man who had two sons. The younger one was very spoiled. He thought his father did not love him because he told him to stay away from his bad friends. He decided to leave home and asked his father for his share of the money. He wanted to inherit his father's money, although his father was still alive.

He took the money and travelled far. He had many parties with his evil friends. He thought he was very happy because he was free to do as he pleased. After a while, all the money was gone and he had to work to eat and live. He tended to pigs, and sometimes, when he was hungry he desired to eat of the bitter food of the pigs while the pigs' owner was not looking.

Finally, he decided to return home and apologize to his father and work for him as a hired servant.

His father saw him from afar and was very happy to see his son return. His father ran toward him. He fell on his neck and kissed him, although he was barefoot, wore torn clothes, and reeked of the smell of pigs, since he had not taken a bath for so long. His father was not ashamed of him and did not rebuke him because he saw that his son's heart was broken. Rather he had a party to celebrate his son's return.

God, our Father in heaven, rejoices, too, and welcomes the return of those who are lost from the Church.

Prayer: Who is your Father in heaven?

The Story of the Lost Coin
Luke 15

Our Lord Jesus also told us a story about a woman who lost a silver coin. The woman cherished this coin. That is why she looked for it everywhere. Finally, she found her lost coin. She called her neighbors and told them to come and celebrate with her because she found her lost coin.

Our Lord Jesus said that, likewise, the angels too rejoice when one sinner repents and joins them in heaven.

Prayer: Let me return to You, Lord, that You may rejoice and celebrate over my return together with the angels.

Our Lord Jesus Raises the Daughter of Jairus
Luke 8

My name is Jairus and I have one little daughter. One day, my daughter became very ill. I ran quickly to look for the Lord Jesus and ask for His help; but when the Lord Jesus came, my little daughter had already died. My wife was beside her and so were our relatives, neighbors, and friends. They were all mourning her. When they saw me, they screamed and I wept. Our Lord Jesus looked at them and at me and said not to weep because she is only asleep. People secretly laughed because they knew she was dead. As for my daughter, the Lord Jesus looked at her and held her hand and told her, "Dear, get up." My daughter immediately got up and asked for something to eat.

How amazing are the things that our Lord Jesus can do. He created us, saved us, and will raise us in the last day that we may live with Him in heaven and never die.

Prayer: Help us, Lord, that we may not be afraid of sickness nor grieve over our loved ones who pass away, and not mourn when we depart from this world.

Our Lord Jesus Calms the Wind
Luke 8

I am Peter, one of the Lord's disciples, and I often accompanied Him. I witnessed a lot of His amazing works. A lot of times, I knew He was the Son of God.

Once, when the evening had come, at the end of a long day, during which our Lord had taught the people about the kingdom of God, He told us to go to the other side of the lake. We all went into the boat. He was tired, so He went to sleep at the back of the boat. We sailed to the middle of the lake of Galilee, but then, a fierce storm blew. High waves hit the boat relentlessly and the water started to fill the boat. We were about to drown, and we became very afraid. We woke the Lord up and told Him, "Teacher, we are drowning. Do you not care? We will all die."

Jesus then rose and told us, "Why are you so afraid like this?" He rebuked the wind and told the sea to cease and be still. Immediately, the wind ceased and became still. We were amazed and told each other, "Who is He? Even the wind and the waves listen to Him and obey Him." Then, we continued sailing until we reached the other side of the lake.

Question: Our Lord Jesus used the wind to show the disciples that nature is under His control because He is the Son of God. How did our Lord quiet the storm?

Our Lord Jesus Walks on Water
Matthew 14

Have you have ever tried to walk on water? Of course, you cannot, but our Lord Jesus can. One evening, after our Lord performed the miracle of feeding the five thousand men and their families with five loaves and two fish, He left us, his disciples, and went up the mountain alone to pray.

He asked us to get into the boat and go ahead of Him to the other shore. In the middle of the night, the wind blew mightily while we were in the middle of the lake. Suddenly, we saw our Lord Jesus walking on the surface of the water of the lake coming toward us. We screamed in terror and thought we were imagining things, but our Lord Jesus comforted us, saying, "Have courage, it is I. Do not be afraid."

Peter could not believe his eyes, so he told our Lord, "If you are He, order me to come down from the boat and walk on water."

Our Lord told him, "Come." Peter stepped down and walked on the water toward our Lord Jesus, but he turned his eyes from our Lord and looked beneath him to see how he is walking on water.

He started to drown and screamed, saying, "Lord, save me." Immediately, our Lord stretched His hand to him and held him.

Our Lord told him, "You of little faith, why did you doubt?"

When they both came into the boat, the wind calmed down and all who were in the boat came and worshipped Him, proclaiming, "You are truly the Son of God."

Jesus did not drown like Peter because He is the Son of God, so He can walk on water. Peter saw our Lord heal the sick, feed the masses, and he was sure that He can do anything; therefore Peter should have continued to believe in our Lord's power, but he allowed fear to get to him and to cause him to lose his faith in our Lord Jesus.

Our Lord Jesus Transfigures on Mount Tabor
Matthew 17

Our Lord Jesus took us (Peter, and the brothers James and John) to climb the high Mount of Tabor. We did not feel tired. We were very happy because we were with Him. When we reached the top of the mountain, our Lord's appearance suddenly changed in front of us and His face lit like the sun so that we could no longer bear to look at Him. His clothes became white like light as if the sun was inside of them. We have never seen a sight like this. We were so surprised that we could not even talk to Him or with each other. Then we saw our Lord Jesus speak to Moses, who received the Law and the Commandments, and to Elijah, who went up to heaven in a chariot of fire. They both lived a long time ago. They were speaking about salvation through the cross. We heard what they said but we did not understand what they meant. Then, we heard a voice coming from the cloud of light in heaven saying, "This is my beloved Son of whom I am well pleased. Hear Him."

We felt we were in heaven itself and that there was nothing more wonderful than what we had seen. That is why the apostle Peter said to our Lord Jesus, "It is good that we are here."

Question: What did the voice from heaven say?

Our Lord Jesus Feeds the Multitude
John 6

We, the apostles of our Lord, will tell you about God's care and providence for the multitudes of His people who followed Him to listen to Him. Our Lord spoke to them about the kingdom of God. He had pity on them and healed the sick. When the day came to an end, we realized that the people became very hungry and there were no places for them to buy food because we were in the wilderness and it was late.

We asked our Lord to let the people leave that they may go to the villages around and buy food, but our Lord refused and told us that there is no need for them to go, "You give them something to eat." We told him we do not have food but that there is a young boy who has five loaves of bread and two fish for his lunch. Jesus said, "Bring them to Me," and ordered everyone to sit in groups. There were about five thousand men, in addition to the women and the children.

The boy brought the food to our Lord. Jesus took the five loaves and two fish and gave thanks. Then, we started to distribute the food. What happened was amazing because everybody ate until they were full. We collected the remainder. There were 12 baskets full of crumbs that remained after all who ate were full.

Question: The little boy gave his lunch to our Lord Jesus. Can you think of something that you can offer to our Lord?

Our Lord Jesus Loves Children
Luke 18

I am Philip, an apostle of our Lord Jesus. I used to accompany Him because I loved Him and because I learned something new from Him every day. Sometimes, I would believe that I am doing the right thing, but later, I would discover that I was wrong.

Jesus loves everyone, especially little children. One day, our Lord was sitting, teaching the people, speaking to them about the kingdom of heaven, and many people gathered around Him as usual. Parents brought their little children so that the Lord would talk to them and bless them, but we tried to prevent them. We told them to go away and that Jesus is very tired.

Jesus heard us and He was not pleased. He asked them to come to Him and said, "Let the children come to Me and do not stop them! For the kingdom of heaven belongs to such as these." He told us that He wished that we would have faith like that of children. He held the children in His arms and played tenderly with them. Sometimes, important people do not give some of their time to children, but when our God became a Man and lived on earth, He spoke to children and gave them of His time because they too are important to Him.

Our Lord asks us to become like children so that we can get into heaven. Jesus loves you too.

Question: What did the disciples of Jesus tell the children? How did Jesus answer His disciples?

The Good Samaritan
Luke 10

Our Lord Jesus told us the following parable that we may know that every human being is like a brother to us. Once, there was a Jewish man going from Jerusalem to Jericho. On the way, he was met by a group of thieves, who took his money and food and beat him up badly. Then, they threw him to the ground seriously injured and left him between life and death. Many of his own people saw him, but they were afraid and did not help him. They abandoned him quickly because they were afraid the thieves would come out to get them.

A Samaritan man passed by him. We know that the Jews used to hate the Samaritans. This man stopped and tended to the Jewish man's wounds. He did not say this is a Jewish man, who hates us, but he thought, this is a brother to me in humanity. That is why this man is called the "good" Samaritan. You also can be "good" by helping everyone from all races and all religions.

Question: Who is your brother?

Our Lord Jesus and the Tax Collector
Luke 19

Do you know me? My name is Zacchaeus. All the Jews, of whom I am one, and all the people of my city, hated me. I did not have any friends. Whenever people saw me from far away, they would leave that road so as not to meet with me. They believed that I was a traitor to my nation and a greedy man because I was the head of tax collection. I used violence to collect more taxes for the enemy—the Roman Empire. I was very rich, but most of my money was earned illegally.

I will tell you how I met our Lord Jesus who changed my life. I used to live in Jericho. One day, Jesus came to our city. I wanted to see Him and tried very hard, but I could not because there were too many people around Him and I am a short man. That is why I ran very quickly and I climbed a sycamore tree on the road so that I could see Jesus. He was going to pass under that tree and nothing was going to stop me from seeing Him. When Jesus came to where I was, He looked up and saw me. He told me, "Zacchaeus, come down immediately. I must stay at your house today."

I quickly came down and embraced Him happily. My heart was bursting with joy. When the people saw this, they were upset and said, "He has gone to be the guest of a sinner."

I stood up and told the Lord, "I will give half of my possessions to the poor, and if I have cheated anybody out of anything, I will pay back four times the amount."

Jesus said to me, "Today salvation has come to this house, because I came to seek and save the lost."

I was very happy with that.

Question: Are you happy because Jesus came to you? Are you ready for Him to stay with you?

Our Lord Jesus and the 10 Lepers
Luke 17

I and nine other people had a horrible disease of the skin. It is called leprosy. I was not Jewish like the other nine. I was a Samaritan. No one was able to help us. Those who suffered from leprosy lived away from everybody because people were afraid to be infected with the disease. The Jews understood leprosy to be a sign of sin. It meant that a person who suffered from leprosy is unclean. Only the Jewish priest was able to decide if a leper is healed and can return to his home and live among his family. One day, Jesus came with His disciples to the village where we lived and we went to receive Him, but we stood afar. We raised our voices saying, "Jesus, have mercy on us; please help us and heal us."

Jesus looked at us and said, "Go and show yourselves to the priests," so we hurried to the priests, and while we were on our way, we were healed. The men ran quickly because they were very happy to be healed, but when I saw that I was healed, I returned to give glory to God with a loud voice. I worshipped Him, and bowed down on my face at the feet of my God Jesus, and thanked Him.

Then Jesus Christ asked, "Did not all ten of you get healed? Where are the other nine? Did no one come back to give glory to God except this man who is a foreigner?" Then He told me, "Get up and go. Your faith has saved you."

The Poor Rich Man
Luke 18

One day, a young rich man asked our Lord Jesus, "How do I inherit the kingdom of heaven?" Jesus knew that this young man loved money more than he loved God. Jesus told him to give his money to the poor and to give his life to God.

Money is a gift from God. Abraham was very rich and he loved God. Joseph of Arimathea was rich and he offered his new tomb, carved in a rock, to Christ so that the body of our Lord Jesus could be buried in it. Lydia was also a rich woman, a seller of purple linen, which was used to make the clothes of kings and great men and she was a believer. Many of the rich kings and leaders and other great men and women loved our Lord Jesus.

As for this young man, he loved riches. For him to enjoy the kingdom of heaven, he had to love God more than he loved money. The young man felt sad and left Jesus and went on his way.

Prayer: Lord, everything I have, You gave me. Open my heart with love that I may be able to give to those in need from Your money that You have given to me.

The Healing of the Man Born Blind
John 9

The disciples saw a blind man and asked, "Master, who sinned, this man or his parents, that he was born blind?"

Jesus answered, "Neither he nor his parents, but that the works of God may be revealed in him." Then, Jesus put a little bit of mud (which he made with some of His spit and dirt) on this man's eyes and told him to wash in the well of Siloam. When the man washed his eyes, he was able to see, and everyone was surprised.

This man was blind. Close your eyes now and imagine that you, too, are blind. Is it not a great blessing that you can see?

Prayer: I thank You, Lord, because You have given me the gift of sight in this life. How much happier will I be when I see Your divine glory?

Our Lord Jesus Meets the Two Sisters
Luke 10

My name is Mary. I lived with my sister, Martha, and my brother, Lazarus, in the city of Bethany, which is two miles away from Jerusalem. We were among the friends of our Lord Jesus. He met with us and came to our house. I sat at His feet and I listened to His words while my sister hurried to the kitchen because she was busy cooking. Martha became upset and complained, "Mary, come and help me."

Jesus corrected Martha and said, "Martha do not be upset. Mary made a better choice to stay with me and listen to what I am saying."

Prayer: Let me be like Mary. Let me come and sit at Your feet and listen to Your voice in the Bible, and let me be like Martha, to serve the poor—Your brothers and sisters.

Raising Lazarus from the Tomb
John 11

My name is Mary and I will tell you how Jesus raised my brother from the dead and returned him to life. One day, my brother, Lazarus, became very sick. My sister and I sent a message to Jesus Christ telling him, "Lord the one you love is sick." When our Lord heard this news, He said, "This sickness is not for death but to show the glory of God."

Jesus remained where He was for two more days and when he came to Bethany, my brother had already passed away four days prior. My sister, Martha, went quickly to meet our Lord when she heard that He was coming, but I stayed in the house with the people who came to offer us condolences. Martha said to Jesus, "Lord, if You had been here, my brother would not have died."

Jesus said to her, "Your brother will rise again."

Martha answered, "I know he will rise again in the resurrection at the last day."

Jesus said to her, "I am the resurrection and the life. The one who believes in Me will live, even though he dies; and whoever lives by believing in Me will never die. Do you believe this?"

"Yes, Lord," she replied, "I believe that You are the Messiah, the Son of God, who is to come into the world."

After this, Martha came to call me, so I got up quickly and came to the Lord Jesus and worshiped at His feet. I wept and told Him, "If you were here my brother would not have died." Everyone around us was crying too. Jesus asked, "Where have you laid him?" We replied, "Come and see, Lord." At this point, Jesus wept and everyone around us saw how Jesus loved Lazarus, my brother.

When we reached the tomb, Jesus said, "Take away the stone." Then, Martha said, "But, Lord, by this time there is a bad odor, for he has been there four days."

Jesus replied, "Did I not tell you that if you believe, you will see the glory of God?"

So, we took away the stone where the dead Lazarus was laid. Then, Jesus looked up and said, "Father, I thank You that You have heard me. I know that You always hear Me."

Then Jesus called with a loud voice, "Lazarus, come out!" The dead man came out, his hands and feet wrapped with strips of linen, and a cloth around his face. Jesus told us, "Take off the grave clothes and let him go." Many of the Jews who saw this believed in Jesus."

Prayer: My Lord Jesus, say a word that I, too, would rise from the tomb of sin.

Our Lord Jesus Goes to Jerusalem
Matthew 21; Luke 19

My name is John and I am one of the close disciples of Jesus. The time that I have spent with Jesus was wonderful. Our Lord Jesus decided to go to Jerusalem to celebrate the Passover Feast and we went with Him. On the road, He told us that He would die soon but we did not understand.

When we came close to Jerusalem near Bethphage and Bethany, Jesus told two of us, "Go to the village ahead of you, and at once you will find a donkey tied there, with her colt by her. Untie them and bring them to Me. If anyone says anything to you, say that the Lord needs them." Those two men went to the village and saw a donkey tied at the gate on the road.

When they untied the donkey, some of the villagers asked them, "Why are you untying the donkey?"

They replied, "The Lord needs it." So, they let them go with it.

They brought it to Jesus and threw their cloaks on it. Jesus sat on it and we all went into Jerusalem.

When the people saw our Lord coming, they greeted Him with their children, rejoicing to receive Him. The children sang joyfully praises to our Lord and the people spread tree branches and their cloaks on the road. They shouted praises: "Hosanna, Blessed is He who comes in the name of the Lord! Hosanna in the highest heaven! Our Lord Jesus is our King."

They wanted Jesus to become their king. When we entered Jerusalem, the whole city was stirred and asked, "Who is this?" Everybody wanted to know who this is that received all this great glory.

Then, we remembered the prophecy of the prophet Zachariah about this event many years ago when he said, "Rejoice Jerusalem, your king comes to you, riding on a donkey, and on a colt" (Zachariah 9)

Prayer: Jesus, come into my heart and stay there that I may rejoice in You and sin can never come near me.

Jesus Clears the Temple
Matthew 21

I am James and a disciple of our Lord Jesus. My God Jesus taught me to love: to love the Father, to love his Holy House, and to love all people.

Our Lord Jesus taught us to respect the house of God. During the Passover Feast, He went with us to Jerusalem. In the temple, we found people selling cows, sheep, and doves. The moneychangers were also sitting there as if it was a marketplace. Our Lord expelled all the traders from the temple and turned the tables of the moneychangers upside down and scattered their coins. He said, "Stop turning My Father's house into a market!"

Question: Our Lord Jesus was upset because the traders were using His holy house to exchange money and trade. Our Lord said that the house of God is a house of prayer. Do you take care of your heart and keep it as a temple of God?

Our Lord Jesus and the Poor Widow
Luke 21

Our Lord Jesus was sitting by the offering box in the temple and rich people were throwing in there a lot of gold coins. A poor widow came and quietly threw in the box all that she owned—two coins of copper. Instead of buying something to eat, she put the two coins in the offering box at the temple. She did that because she loved God a lot. Jesus our Lord explained that she had given much more than the rich people who offered gold because she offered everything she had with love, but the rich people had given very little of their money with pride and bragging. The disciples were surprised.

Question: What do you offer to God in private with love and humility?

Plotting Against Our Lord Jesus
Matthew 26

Some of the leaders of Jerusalem hated our Lord Jesus so they plotted to kill Him. They schemed to arrest Him.

Our Lord Jesus was humble. He dressed like His disciples and never tried to stand out among them. That is why the leaders of Jerusalem were afraid that they would mistakenly arrest one of His disciples and He would run away.

Therefore, they talked with Judas, originally one of the twelve disciples, who was in charge of keeping the money box of all the disciples. These leaders gave Judas 30 pieces of silver to help them arrest Jesus in the garden of Gethsemane while He was with His disciples.

Question: Do you pray that you do not fall into temptation that would lead you away from your Savior?

The First Divine Liturgy
Luke 22

At night, Jesus ate the Jewish Passover dinner with His disciples and told them again, "I will soon die," but still they did not understand.

Our Lord took a big towel and started to wash and wipe the feet of His disciples. Slaves usually washed the feet of their masters, but great men did not usually accept to wash the feet of others.

While they were eating, Judas snuck out to go meet the men who were plotting against our Lord Jesus.

The Lord Jesus took bread and wine and blessed them, divided them, and gave them to His disciples. He confirmed, "This is My body that has been broken for you and for many and this is My blood that has been poured out for you and for many. Do this in remembrance of Me." Our Lord Jesus told His disciples that soon the Jews would bring the soldiers to arrest Him and then kill Him.

Our Lord Jesus died on the cross to save us. He truly loves us and He became Man to be crucified for us.

Question: How do you return Christ's love since He allows you to partake of the Holy Communion (the "Eucharist," which is a word that means thanksgiving)?

In the Garden
Luke 22; John 18

After establishing the Divine Liturgy, our Lord Jesus took His disciples to the garden of Gethsemane and said, "Let us pray." But they all slept. So, our Lord Jesus prayed to His Father. Night fell and it became pitch dark. Jesus knew that He would soon die for our sins. He was ready to die because this was the will of the Father. He specifically came to the world to die for us. He told us that we ought to follow His example. We must do the will of God in our lives.

Suddenly, lots of voices were heard. It was Judas coming with those who opposed our Lord Jesus. The disciples woke up from their sleep and were very afraid, so they fled. Jesus asked the soldiers, "Who do you seek," and they responded, "Jesus." When the Lord responded, "I am He," they immediately fell to the ground. Jesus surrendered to the soldiers who violently bound Him with ropes. They thought He needed to be bound like this so He would not run away. They led Him at night to the house of the high priest to sentence Him to death.

What happened then was very saddening. The Jews and the soldiers came to take Jesus, but His disciples fled because they were afraid. No one tried to help Him.

Question: Why did our Lord Jesus not flee from the soldiers when they fell to the ground in front of Him?

Judged by the Priests
Luke 22; John 18

Caiaphas, the high priest that year, advised them to take Jesus to the palace of his father-in-law, Annas, who was highly respected because of his age and popularity, so that the people would feel that Annas and Caiaphas both agree to wanting Jesus to be judged. The soldiers led Jesus to Annas first, and Peter and John followed from afar to watch what was going to happen to their Master. John knew the high priest, so he was able to get into the house while Peter did not dare to do say but instead stayed with the servants outside. A servant girl looked closely at him and told him, "You are one of His disciples."

Peter was frightened and responded, "What are you saying? I do not know Him at all." Peter was afraid that the servant may tell the high priest on him and they would arrest him and kill him, too. That is why he said, "not me."

A while later, some people came and told Peter, "You are one of them, too. Your accent betrays you." Peter began to swear that he does not know the Man. He also denied Jesus a third time before the rooster crowed. At this moment, Jesus looked toward him. Peter saw in Jesus's look a rebuke and an invitation to repent for what he did. Peter, then, remembered what the Master had told him that he would deny Christ three times before the rooster crows twice. Peter went outside the palace and wept with bitterness. He never forgot the Master's look when he denied Him and cursed and swore. Although Peter loved Jesus and did not want to deny Him, Peter fell into this sin because he was weak. He regretted it bitterly.

Our Lord Jesus forgave him and Peter started to evangelize to people and tell them about Jesus.

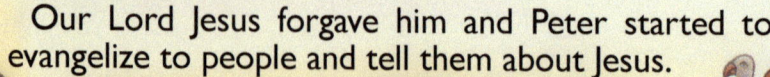

Judged by the Civil Court
Luke 23

In the early morning, Pontius Pilate saw a group of Jewish priests and elders coming toward his palace bringing a tied up man. When Pilate asked them why they brought this man, they said, "We found him inciting the people and preventing them from paying taxes to Caesar. He also said that he is the king, the Messiah."

Pilate decided to send Him to Herod the king, ruler of Galilee, who happened to be in Jerusalem at the time.

Herod was very happy when he saw Jesus because he heard a lot about Him and wished to see Jesus perform a miracle in front of him. He asked Jesus a lot of questions to spare Him a crucifixion sentence; however, our Lord did not answer. Finally, when the chief priests and scribes vehemently complained against Jesus, Herod and his soldiers ridiculed and mocked the Lord. Herod dressed Jesus in bright clothes and sent Him back to Pilate. From that moment onward, the two enemies, Pontius Pilate and Herod, reconciled and became friends.

Our Lord Jesus sent a dream to Pilate's wife that upset her all night and she in turn warned her husband from taking a position against our Lord Jesus. Therefore, the Roman ruler said, "This man did not do anything that deserves death," and wanted to set Him free. It was the custom to release a prisoner during every feast. Pontius Pilate asked the people if he should release Jesus, but the Jews preferred to crucify our Lord Jesus, and instead, to release Barabbas, the thief. The people started to cry out, "Crucify Him; crucify Him." Pilate ordered that the soldiers do as the people had asked. The soldiers took our Lord Jesus and nailed Him to a wooden cross and left Him to die. The disciples and their friends were very sad because they lost someone very dear to them.

Prayer: You have accepted with Your free will to be crucified for me. Holy One, make me holy so that I may not crucify You with my sins another time.

Our Lord Jesus on the Cross
Luke 23

The soldiers crucified our Lord Jesus on the wood of the cross. They nailed His hands and His feet, and they crucified beside Him two thieves, one on His right and one on His left. The thief on the right repented for his sins and asked our Lord to forgive him and to remember him once He is in His kingdom.

Our Lord Jesus told him, "Today you will be with Me in paradise."

Our Lord Jesus forgives those who repent, regret their sins, and seek forgiveness.

The thief on the right did not see our Lord Jesus while He was performing countless miracles nor did he see His transfiguration on Mount Tabor nor did he hear the words of the angel to the shepherds.

He only saw Christ crucified, and how Christ looked lovingly toward those who crucified Him. Having seen that the right hand thief believed that Jesus was the Messiah, the King, who loves mankind and he loved Him back and wished to be with Jesus in His eternal kingdom.

The Jews asked that Jesus be crucified and die. Why did they kill Him? Did He do any anything bad? He died because of the sins that we, you and I, do.

Question: Why did our Lord Jesus die?

Our Lord Jesus Is Alive!
Luke 24

When Jesus died, His disciples buried Him in a new tomb and rolled a big rock in front of the entrance of the tomb. The Jews asked Pilate to seal the tomb so that no one would dare to come and roll the rock away from the entrance.

Early Sunday morning, some women went to the tomb with the spices they prepared. They found the rock rolled away and two angels sitting inside the tomb. The angels said to them, "Do not be afraid. Our Lord Jesus is alive. He has risen from death."

Early Sunday morning, our Lord Jesus rose from the dead, while the rock was still in its place, and the guards were terrified.

Our Lord came out of the tomb alive and sent an angel to roll the rock away so that the women and the disciples would be sure that He has risen from the dead.

Believers later started to greet one another saying, "Christ is risen," and answer back to each other by saying, "Truly He is risen."

Question: Where did Jesus go when He gave up the Spirit?

Two Disciples Meet Our Lord Jesus
Luke 24

When our Lord Jesus had risen from the dead, it happened that two of His disciples were returning to Jerusalem from Emmaus. They were very sad because Jesus, who raised the dead and whom they had hoped was the Messiah, had died.

Jesus wanted to comfort them, so He walked along with them while they were returning to the village. At first, they did not know Him and thought He was a stranger. They told Him, "We were hoping that Jesus would be the one to save Israel. It is now three days since Jesus had died and some women have astonished us because they went to the tomb early in the morning and did not find His body. They returned saying that they saw angels who said He was alive. Some of us went to the tomb and found as the women reported but did not see Jesus." When the two men arrived at the house, they invited the Stranger [Jesus—not yet revealed to them] to have dinner with them. When they laid the food down, He sat with them and took bread, blessed it, broke it, and gave it to them. At that moment, their eyes opened and they knew Him. Then, He disappeared. The men realized that the Stranger was our Lord Jesus. He is truly alive!

How happy they were when they knew that Jesus had risen from the dead! They were so joyful that they ran quickly to Jerusalem to tell their friends.

Question: Why were the two disciples of Jesus sad?

Last Breakfast on the Shore
John 21

I am Peter. I used to earn my living by fishing. I will tell you about my last fishing trip. One day, after our Lord Jesus had risen from the dead, I went to fish with some of the disciples of our Lord Jesus. We tried all night, but we did not catch any fish. In the morning, our Lord Jesus was on the shore and we did not know that it was Him. He asked us, "Do you have food?" When we answered that we do not have any, He told us to throw the net to the right side of the boat and we will find fish.

We threw the net in the water as He said, and the net was filled with fish—153 big fish. We were not able to pull the net because of the many fish that were caught. Then, John told me, "It is the Lord!" When I heard what John said I threw myself in the water and swam to the shore. Jesus had prepared fish on a fire pit and some bread. I went back to the boat to help my friends pull the net to the land. Jesus took the bread and the fish and He gave it to us.

After we had eaten, our Lord Jesus said to Simon (Peter), "Simon son of Jonah do you love Me more than these?" I answered, "Yes, my Lord. You know that I love You," and Jesus responded, "Tend My sheep." Then, He asked me a second time, "Simon son of Jonah do you love Me?" I answered, "Yes, my Lord," and He again said, "Tend My sheep." He then asked me a third time, "Simon, son of Jonah, do you love Me?" I replied, "My Lord, You know everything; You know how much I love You." Then, Jesus told me, "Tend My sheep." I previously denied my Lord Jesus three times and now three times I told him I love Him. That is why I spent the rest of my life speaking to people about our Lord.

Prayer: You know how much I love You, although I confess to You that I am the first among sinners.

Our Lord Jesus Ascends to Heaven
Luke 24; Acts 1

Some of Jesus's disciples, especially Thomas, did not easily believe that our Lord Jesus had risen from the dead and returned back to life. That is why our Lord Jesus showed them the marks of the nails in His hands and feet. For 40 days, the disciples were assured that He is alive forever because He appeared to many of them several times and He spoke about things that concerned the kingdom of heaven.

While He was meeting with them, He told them not to leave Jerusalem but to wait for the Father's timing, which He had explained to them earlier, and that they will receive power once the Holy Spirit descends upon them, and they will be witnesses for Him in Jerusalem, all Judea, Samaria, and unto the end of the earth. While He was saying these things, He started ascending. The disciples watched Jesus ascend until a cloud hid Him from their eyes. Meanwhile, two men dressed in white were standing there and said to us, "Men of Galilee, why are you standing like this, looking toward heaven? Jesus has ascended to heaven and He will come back again the same way as you have seen Him ascend."

Look at what is happening: Jesus is ascending to heaven. He is going to heaven where His Father is. He is saying goodbye to His disciples, but He is also telling them that He will be coming again and that they will be always and forever with Him. We, too, will be with Him.

Then, the disciples returned to Jerusalem in great joy.

Question: Why did the disciples return to Jerusalem in great joy? Did they think that they would no longer see Jesus?

The Descent of the Holy Spirit
Acts 2

After our Lord Jesus ascended to heaven and while His apostles were sitting together with many disciples and friends, a loud voice from heaven, like the blowing of a violent wind, was heard. Tongues of fire rested on each one of them, but the fire did not burn them. It is the Spirit of the Holy God that descended upon them and resided in their hearts. The Holy Spirit helps us and teaches us faith in our Lord Jesus Christ.

After that happened, the people spoke in many languages that they had not known before. Soon, the news spread and many people came from different countries—Parthians, Medes and Elamites, residents of Mesopotamia, Judea and Cappadocia, Pontus and Asia, Phrygia and Pamphylia, Egypt and parts of Libya, Romans, Cretans, and Arabs—and each one heard everyone else speaking in their own language, declaring the wonders of God.

Question: Did God accept their many prayers and requests for the Church in the whole world?

Saint Peter and Saint John Help a Lame Man
Acts 3

One day, Saint Peter and Saint John went to the temple to pray. There was a lame man, who was not able to walk, sitting outside the temple asking for alms. They told him, "We do not have money, but in the name of Jesus, get up and walk." The man got up and started praising God. This man was unable to walk since birth; however, not only was he able to walk now, but he was also able to jump with joy. What happened? Saint Peter and Saint John, the two disciples of Jesus, ordered his illness to go away, in the name of Jesus.

The Holy Spirit gave them the power to heal this man's illness. The lame man did not think to rush home to tell his family, but he immediately went into the temple to thank God and praise Him before he thanked the two disciples.

Question: What do you do when the Lord gives you a good gift?

The Deacon Saint Stephen—The First Martyr
Acts 7

Saint Stephen never stopped telling people about how much our Lord Jesus loves all humanity. He told the people that Jesus, about whom the prophets had spoken, has come and has been crucified on behalf of the whole world and that only He can forgive sins. This angered the Jews who did not love Jesus the Lord. Saint Stephen's face shone like that of an angel.

When the Jews heard what he said, they were very upset with him. Saint Stephen looked toward heaven and he was filled with the Holy Spirit. He saw Jesus standing in heaven. Saint Stephen said, "I can see the heavens open and the Son of Man standing at the right hand of God." When he said this, the Jews threw stones at him until he died. Saint Stephen went to Paradise to be with his Savior Jesus Christ.

Deacon Stephen was the first martyr and he showed us that the work of the deacons is not only to take care of the hymns and teach them in church, but also to teach the Bible and to be a witness by example, behavior, thoughts, and words to our Lord Jesus who saved us.

Question: Why were these people angry with Saint Stephen, the deacon?

A Man from Ethiopia Hears about Our Lord Jesus Christ
Acts 8

The Minister of the Ethiopian Queen was in his chariot driven by fast horses back to his country returning from Jerusalem. He was reading the Book of Isaiah in the Holy Bible out loud.

On his way, he met Philip, one of the disciples of our Lord Jesus Christ. God had sent Philip to speak to this man and to help him understand what he was reading.

The man told Philip, "I wish to be baptized and be a son of God."

Philip answered, "If you believe with all your heart, it is possible."

He answered, "I believe that Jesus Christ is the Son of God." The minister ordered that the chariot be stopped and together with Philip, they got off the chariot and went to the water where he was baptized. Then, the Spirit of God carried Philip away and the man no longer saw him.

The minister was happy to be baptized because he received a new spiritual birth and became Christian.

Prayer: Send me, Lord, to tell the people about You all the days of my life and to rejoice in those who return to You.

Saul of Tarsus Meets Our Lord Jesus
Acts 9

Saul of Tarsus did not believe that our Lord Jesus is the Son of God. He used to kill those who believed in Jesus. He hated the name of Jesus and His Church. Saul thought that he was serving God by killing Christians. One day, while he was going to Damascus to arrest those who believed in our Lord Jesus Christ, a bright light in the sky suddenly appeared to him while he was on the road. He fell to the ground and he heard a voice from heaven. It was the voice of our Lord Jesus Christ calling upon him by name saying, "Saul, Saul, why are you persecuting me?" Saul did not think that he was persecuting anyone wrongly, but he thought that God, Himself, and all the heavenly beings were happy with him because he killed the Christians.

Saul said, "Who are you, Sir?"

God replied, "I am Jesus whom you persecute. It is difficult for you to fight Me." Christ also told him, "I am Jesus and you hurt Me because you hurt those who believe in Me." After this, Saul became one of the disciples of our Lord Jesus Christ and his name was changed to Paul. He began to tell people in many countries about the cross of our Lord Jesus and about His resurrection and ascension to the heavens. Paul longed to tell everybody that Jesus is the Son of God, the Savior of the world. Paul was completely changed!

Question: The Church used to pray for Saul who persecuted it. Do you pray for those in the world who persecute the Church? Do you pray for those who persecute the Church today in the entire world?

Saint Paul Preaches in Damascus
Acts 9

Many people believed in our Lord Jesus when Paul preached to them in Damascus, but some people wanted to kill him. They used to watch the gates of the city of Damascus night and day so they could kill him when he leaves through the gates. That is why his friends and disciples took him at night and they put him in a big basket, which they lowered from the walls of the city until he reached the ground outside Damascus in peace.

Question: Were the people who did not like Saint Paul able to stop him from preaching in many countries?

Saint Peter Preaches to Cornelius
Acts 10

There was a man named Cornelius. He was a Centurion in the Roman army. Most of the Roman soldiers were known to be violent, but Cornelius was a good, God-fearing man. Together with his family, he did a lot of good deeds for the people and prayed to God at all times because he wanted to know more about Him. God sent him an angel to tell him where to find Saint Peter so that Saint Peter may tell him about God. Cornelius sent three of his servants to bring Saint Peter to him in his house. Saint Peter went to him with a group of friends. Cornelius also invited his relatives and friends.

When Saint Peter arrived, Cornelius fell on his face at his feet. Saint Peter told him, "Get up, I too am a man." Cornelius welcomed Saint Peter with a lot of people and told him that he has been fasting for four days until this hour, and at 9 o'clock while he was praying in his house, an angel appeared to him in bright clothing and told him: "Cornelius, God has heard your prayer and remembered your gifts to the poor. Send some people to Joppa for Simon who is called Peter to come to you. He is a guest in the home of Simon the tanner, who lives by the sea. He will talk to you when he comes."

Saint Peter talked to them about our Lord Jesus and told them that Jesus is able to forgive their sins. They believed in the Lord Jesus and were baptized. This was the first group of Gentiles (non-Jews) to be baptized.

Question: Why did God send an angel to guide Cornelius to bring Saint Peter?

Saint Peter Is Released from Jail
Acts 12

Saint Peter started to preach to people in Jerusalem. He said, "Our Lord Jesus loved us and died for us and He is alive!" However, the enemies of our Lord Jesus did not accept what Saint Peter was saying or doing. King Herod arrested him and put him in prison. He delivered him into the hands of soldiers: four groups of several soldiers worked at different times to make sure he would not escape. Herod intended to deliver Saint Peter to the people after the Passover Feast to sentence him to death.

While Saint Peter was in prison, the Church was diligently praying to God for him. In the middle of the night, an angel of the Lord came to Saint Peter in prison and woke him up. The angel told him, "Get up." In the same moment, his chains with which he was tied fell to the ground and the doors of the prison opened without keys. Saint Peter walked out of prison a free man. On the way, Saint Peter, who thought he was dreaming, came to himself and said, "Now I know without a doubt that the Lord has sent his angel and rescued me from the hand of Herod and from everything the Jewish people were hoping would happen to me." He went to the house of Mary the mother of John, whose last name is Mark, where many people had gathered and were praying. Peter knocked at the outer entrance, and a servant named Rhoda came to answer the door. When she recognized Peter's voice, she was so overjoyed that she ran back without opening it and said, "Peter is at the door!" "You are out of your mind," the peole in the house told her. When she kept insisting that it was true, they said, "It must be his angel." Peter kept knocking, and when they opened the door and saw him, they were in disbelief.

Prayer: Lord, remember those who are imprisoned and who suffer unjustly and those who have no one to ask about them.

King Herod or Saint Peter
Acts 12

Saint Peter enjoyed a heavenly vision and went to Cornelius the Centurion and Gentile (non-Jew) to tell him and his household about it. Saul of Tarsus [Saint Paul the Apostle] also enjoyed a vision of our Lord Jesus, Himself, in which he was told that he would be a chosen vessel to preach the good news of Christ to the Gentiles. The devil, the enemy of all good, was so unhappy about that, so he wanted King Herod to arrest and kill the disciple James, the bishop of Jerusalem. Herod also wanted to arrest and harm the rest of the disciples.

Meanwhile, service in Antioch grew at the hands of Saint Barnabas and Saint Paul, and Antioch was able to support Jerusalem. However, war came from the outside. King Herod was angry with the people of Tyre and Sidon. They joined together and asked to speak with him. On the appointed day, Herod, wearing his royal robes, sat on his throne and with pride delivered a public speech to the people. They shouted, "This is the voice of a god, not of a man." Immediately, because Herod did not give praise to God, an angel of the Lord struck him down, and he was eaten by worms and died. With his death, the word of God spread and many believed in the Gospel of our Lord Jesus.

Barnabas and Paul returned to Jerusalem from Antioch after they had finished their service and took with them John, who is also known as Saint Mark the Apostle.

Question: Can the devil and his evil helpers resist Christ's Church?

The Two Saints, Paul and Barnabas, Go on a Missionary Trip
Acts 13

Saint Paul wanted to tell the people about our Lord Jesus. He met Saint Barnabas and they became friends. They walked many miles together, and wherever they went, they talked to the people about our Lord Jesus, His love for mankind, His crucifixion, and His resurrection.

Do you remember Saint Paul? He has now become a disciple of our Lord Jesus. He took many journeys, sometimes by boat, and sometimes on foot. He travelled from one town to the next talking about our Lord Jesus. He told people about the love of our Lord Jesus Christ for them. You, too, can witness to our Lord Jesus everyday.

Question: Do you pray for those who upset you? Do you wish for people to know about our Lord Jesus?

Saint Timothy, the Disciple of Saint Paul
Acts 16, 2 Timothy 1

Both Timothy's mother and grandmother, Eunice and Lois, were Jewish women who loved God very much. They were sure that our Lord Jesus loved them, too, and that He died on the cross for our sins, and that He forgives our sins. They taught Timothy about the Christian faith when he was young. That is why he gave his life to our Lord Jesus and announced that he will always be an obedient son to Him.

Timothy's grandmother read for him a story from the Holy Bible every night. When Timothy grew up, he became a disciple of Saint Paul the apostle. He told many people about our Savior Jesus Christ.

Question: Do you have your own copy of the Holy Bible? Do you read in it every night like Saint Timothy? Do you want to tell people about Jesus like Saint Timothy? Do you try to tell the good news about Jesus in your house, and with your friends at school, and in church like Saint Timothy?

Saint Paul and Lydia, the Purple Seller
Acts 16

A group of God-fearing Jewish women met at the riverside in a city called Philippi to pray and worship God. Saint Paul told them everything about our Lord Jesus and that He is the Son of God, the Savior of the world. He explained to them the prophecies of the Old Testament, which foretold about Christ, beginning with Adam and until the coming of John the Baptist in the New Testament.

One of those Jewish women, Lydia, had faith in God but had not heard about Jesus. She was very rich because she sold purple coloring, which was used to make the clothes of kings and great men. When Saint Paul told her about Jesus, she believed that He is the Son of God.

Question: Do you know that the prophet Isaiah prophesied about the coming of Christ the Savior 700 years before Jesus was actually born?

Saint Paul and Saint Silas in Prison
Acts 16

Saint Paul and Saint Silas went to many places together preaching the Gospel.

In one city, they were sent to prison although they did nothing wrong. They only preached to the people and told them about our Lord Jesus. Even in prison, they prayed and praised God. Suddenly, one midnight as they praised the Lord, God sent a great earthquake. The earth started to shake. The shackles fell off the hands of the prisoners, and the locked prison gates opened, but the two saints did not run away. The prison guard was terrified because he thought they ran away, but Saint Paul called on him and reassured him that they were still there and have not run away.

The guard could not believe what he heard and saw and asked them how he, too, can follow Christ. The guard believed and took Paul and Silas to his house where they spoke to him and to his household about God. They all believed and were baptized. The next day, the guard released them and they were able to go talk to the people about our Lord Jesus.

Question: Why was the guard not afraid of receiving Paul and Silas in his house?

Saint Paul Meets Aquila and His Wife Priscilla
Acts 18

Saint Paul met Aquila and his wife Priscilla. They were tentmakers, and so was Paul. He told them everything about our Lord Jesus. They believed in our Lord Jesus Christ and accompanied Saint Paul. They travelled from city to city preaching the Gospel of Jesus Christ to the people. Saint Paul stayed with them and earned his living working with his hands, making tents for shepherds and soldiers. Aquila and Priscilla turned their home into a small church where they received the believers and worshipped the Lord.

Apollos, a good speaker, and a highly educated man, came to Ephesus. He was known for his interesting talks on any topic, and he interpreted the Holy Bible. He knew about God, His work, and His teachings but Apollo's knowledge was limited to the baptism of John the Baptist who came to pave the way for our Lord by being a voice crying out in the wilderness. It seems Apollos did not hear about our Lord Jesus, His crucifixion, His resurrection and His ascension to heavens, nor did he hear about the descent of the Holy Spirit on the Church. He had received the baptism of Saint John the Baptist but did not enjoy the baptism in the name of Jesus Christ and did not receive the Holy Spirit. When Aquila and Priscilla heard him speak in the synagogue, they realized the limits of his knowledge concerning our Lord Jesus, so they encouraged him and explained to him what he did not know. As a result, he became a successful preacher and a caring teacher who publicly and fearlessly spoke about the coming of Christ the Lord.

Question: Lord, grant me the humility of Apollos, who although was a good speaker, highly educated, and famous, listened to Aquila and Priscilla, believed in the baptism of our Lord Jesus Christ, and preached about the work of the Holy Spirit.

Saint Paul Is Imprisoned a Second Time
Acts 25–27

Once more, Saint Paul returned to Jerusalem where he was thrown again into prison for preaching about Jesus Christ. When he was sent to the king, Saint Paul told him, "I did nothing wrong. I just spoke to the people about our Lord Jesus—the Immortal One." Saint Paul raised his case to Caesar, so that he may preach the Gospel in the Imperial Palace and in Rome. Saint Paul took a long sea journey to reach Rome. Suddenly, a storm blew and the ship was endangered, but an angel told Paul, "The Lord has granted you the lives of all those travelling with you. None of them will be hurt."

The winds blew harder and the waves grew higher, and finally, the ship drowned but Saint Paul and the travelers were safe. They continued to swim. God preserved Saint Paul and the travelers who were with him because of Saint Paul's prayers. They swam until they reached land. God did not want Saint Paul to die yet, because he wanted him to continue preaching. God wanted Saint Paul to tell everybody about our Lord Jesus.

Question: Did tribulations prevent Saint Paul from preaching about God? Why did the angel reassure Saint Paul that God had granted him the lives of his fellow travellers although they were pagans (non-Christians)?

Saint Paul Imprisoned in Rome
Acts 28

Saint Paul was imprisoned in Rome and stayed there for a very long time. This time, however, God did not send an earthquake or an angel to release him like He did with Saint Peter. God still loved Saint Paul as He loved him as always, but He left him there so that he can witness to our Lord, His savior, when he would stand for trial in the royal palace, and would gain some members of the royal house for Christ.

Sometimes, God allows problems to happen but He loves us at all times.

Question: Do you believe that all things work for good for those who love God?

Our Lord Jesus Reveals to Saint John Details about His Next Coming
Revelation 1

Saint John the Apostle was one of the disciples of our Lord Jesus and was very close to Him. Our Lord loved him very much.

When Saint John grew old, our Lord Jesus appeared to him in a vision. Saint John saw the Lord in heaven. Our Lord Jesus revealed to him the events that will happen on the day of His next coming when Christ comes to judge the living and dead. The best thing that He revealed is that He will come soon and will take with Him all those who believe in Him to the kingdom of heaven. Saint John wrote everything he saw in his vision in a book called, "Revelation," the last book of the New Testament in the Holy Bible.

Question: What did Saint John see in his vision?

www.ingramcontent.com/pod-product-compliance
Lightning Source LLC
Chambersburg PA
CBHW042326150426
43193CB00001B/1